W9-BMM-921

Rescue-Mania!

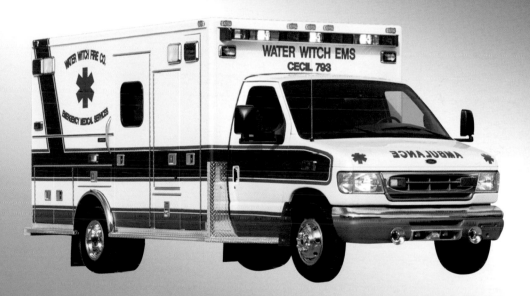

By Caroline Bingham

Gareth Stevens Publishing

A WORLD ALMANAC EDUCATION GROUP COMPANY

Please visit our web site at: www.garethstevens.com
For a free color catalog describing Gareth Stevens Publishing's list
of high-quality books and multimedia programs, call 1-800-542-2595 (USA)
or 1-800-387-3178 (Canada). Gareth Stevens Publishing's fax: (414) 332-3567.

Library of Congress Cataloging-in-Publication Data

Bingham, Caroline, 1962-
    Rescue-mania! / by Caroline Bingham. — North American ed.
        p. cm. — (Vehicle-mania!)
    Includes index.
    Contents: Striker 4500 fire engine — Bronto Skylift fire truck — Heavy Rescue 56 truck — Medtec Saturn ambulance —
R44 helicopter — Super Huey helicopter — P-3 Orion air tanker — Fire Dart fireboat — Atlantic 75 lifeboat —
HH-60J Jayhawk — LR7 rescue submersible — Hagglunds BV206 — Marine Protector.
        ISBN 0-8368-3784-3 (lib. bdg.)
        1. Emergency vehicles—Juvenile literature.   2. Rescue work—Juvenile literature.   [1. Emergency vehicles.   2. Rescue work.]
I. Title.   II. Series.
    TL235.8.B58   2003
    629.225—dc21   2003043916

This North American edition first published in 2004 by
Gareth Stevens Publishing
A World Almanac Education Group Company
330 West Olive Street, Suite 100
Milwaukee, Wisconsin 53212

This U.S. edition copyright © 2004 by Gareth Stevens Inc. Original edition copyright © 2003 ticktock Entertainment Ltd.
First published in Great Britain in 2003 by ticktock Media Ltd., Unit 2, Orchard Business Centre, North Farm Road,
Tunbridge Wells, Kent, TN2 3XF, United Kingdom.

We would like to thank: Tim Bones and Elizabeth Wiggans.

Gareth Stevens Editors: Betsy Rasmussen and Jim Mezzanotte
Gareth Stevens Art Direction: Tammy Gruenewald

Photo credits: Alamy: 9b, 19t, 26-27c; Bronto: 1bl, 6-7; Check-6 images: 1cr, 8-9c, 14-15, 26c; Jane's Defence Weekly:
28-29c; London Fire Authority: 19-20c; Oshkosh: 3bl, 4-5, 10-11, 31b; Perry Slingsby Systems: 3br, 24-25c, 30b; RNLI:
20-21; Robinson Helicopters: 12-13; Sylvia Corday Photo Library: 25t; U.S. Coastguard: 2, 16-17, 22-23, 29t, 30t.

Printed in Hong Kong

1 2 3 4 5 6 7 8 9 07 06 05 04 03

CONTENTS

STRIKER 4500 FIRE ENGINE

Did You Know?

Airport fire engines use **foam** instead of water to put out fast-spreading fuel fires.

The Striker 4500 is a giant fire engine used to put out fires at airports. It is the largest fire engine in the world. The Striker has a huge water tank that can hold as much water as nine ordinary fire engines.

The Striker has huge wheels. The wheels keep the Striker's **body** high off the ground, so the vehicle can travel easily over muddy soil and get to a fire as quickly as possible.

The Striker has a special tool called a snozzle on the end of its **boom**. If an aircraft catches fire, the snozzle pierces a hole in the aircraft's body, and a camera on the end looks inside. The snozzle then squirts foam onto the fire.

FACTS AND STATS

First Model Year: 2002

Origin: United States

Size of Crew: 5 people

Length: 45 feet (13.6 meters)

Width: 10 feet (3 m)

Height: 11 feet (3.5 m)

Weight:
44 tons (40 metric tons)

Fuel Capacity:
70 gallons (265 liters)

Water Tank Capacity:
4,500 gallons (17,033 l)

Foam Tank Capacity:
630 gallons (2,385 l)

Maximum Power:
950 **horsepower** (hp)

Maximum Speed:
50 miles (80 kilometers) per hour

The sprayers are controlled by a joystick inside the cab.

BRONTO SKYLIFT FIRE TRUCK

Did You Know?

The Bronto's aerial platform can also be used like a **crane**. It can lift a person on a stretcher out of a building.

The Bronto Skylift has the tallest **aerial** platform in the world. It is used to put out fires in very tall buildings. It can reach high enough to rescue people on the thirty-third floor of a skyscraper.

The aerial platform of the latest model of the Bronto Skylift can reach up to 236 feet (72 m).

FACTS AND STATS

First Model Year: 2000

Origin: Finland

Size of Crew: 5 people

Length: 49 feet (15 m)

Width: 8 feet (2.5 m)

Height: 13 feet (3.9 m)

Weight:
52 tons (47.5 m tons)

Maximum Load:
882 pounds
(400 kilograms)

Fuel Capacity:
70 gallons (265 l)

Water Discharge Capacity:
1,004 gallons (3,800 l)
per minute

Maximum Power: 480 hp

Maximum Speed:
40 miles (64 km) per hour

The Bronto has a thick steel hose. The hose unfolds with the steel boom when the boom is extended.

The aerial platform can be controlled from the ground or by a firefighter on the platform.

HEAVY RESCUE 56 TRUCK

This amazing vehicle is used by the Los Angeles Fire Department. It is called to accidents that need cutting or heavy lifting capabilities. The Heavy Rescue 56 is used at various emergencies, from traffic accidents to collapsed buildings.

The boom on the Heavy Rescue can be swung to the side to lift a vehicle out of a ditch or a river.

Did You Know?

In dangerous situations, the Heavy Rescue's lifting boom can be operated by **remote control** from 500 feet (152 m) away.

Legs called **outriggers** steady the truck as the **winch** is used. Each outrigger can be moved to stabilize the vehicle if it is on uneven ground.

FACTS AND STATS

First Model Year: 1995

Origin: United States

Size of Crew: 5 people

Length: 32 feet (10 m)

Width: 10 feet (3 m)

Height: 11 feet (3.5 m)

Weight:
48,510 pounds (22,000 kg)

Maximum Load:
80,000 pounds (36,288 kg)

Fuel Capacity:
80 gallons (299 l)

Maximum Power: 460 hp

Maximum Speed:
100 miles (160 km) per hour

Gears: 18 forward, 4 reverse

This vehicle's winch has 295 feet (90 m) of thick steel cable. It is strong enough to lift something that weighs as much as fifteen cars.

MEDTEC SATURN AMBULANCE

Ambulances carry lifesaving equipment to accident victims. They rush to the scene and provide emergency treatment. Then they strap victims to stretchers and take them to the nearest hospital.

Did You Know?

The first ambulances were horse-drawn wagons. Motorized ambulances were first used in the early twentieth century.

Some of the Saturn's lifesaving equipment is electrically powered. The ambulance carries a **battery pack** powerful enough to operate this machinery.

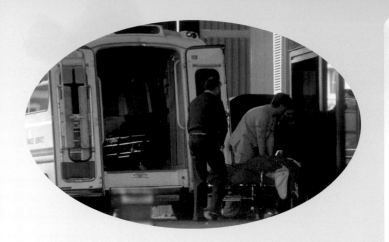

Double rear doors allow stretchers to be loaded easily. The Saturn also has room for more than two hundred items of equipment.

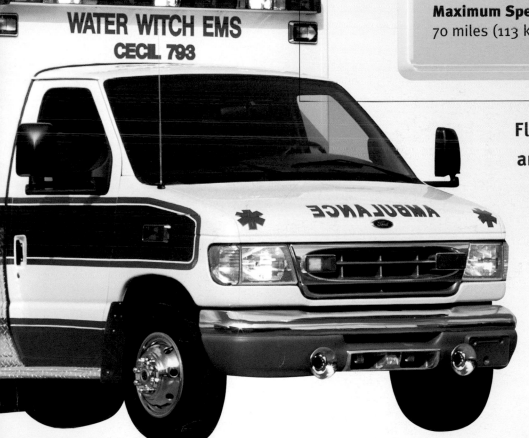

WATER WITCH EMS
CECIL 793

AMBULANCE

Flashing lights are recognized around the world as the sign of an emergency vehicle.

R44 HELICOPTER

This four-seat helicopter is an "eye in the sky" for police forces. It has special equipment to help police carry out their work. At night, for example, its **infrared camera** allows the police to film from above what is happening on the ground.

Did You Know?

The R44 has a special link that lets the helicopter crew send live video images to police on the ground.

Large windows allow clear vision from all of the seats. The **cabin** is also padded with special foam to reduce **engine** noise inside.

Helicopters carry less fuel than airplanes, so they cannot travel as far without stopping to refuel. The R44 can travel 400 miles (644 km) on one tank of fuel — a long distance for a helicopter.

FACTS AND STATS

First Model Year: 1993

Origin: United States

Size of Crew: 4 people

Length:
39 feet (12 m)

Height:
11 feet (3.5 m)

Weight:
1,442 pounds (654 kg)

Maximum Load:
957 pounds (434 kg)

Fuel Capacity:
31 gallons (116 l)

Maximum Power:
1,500 hp

Cruising Speed:
130 miles (209 km) per hour

Maximum Flying Height:
14,000 feet (4,267 m)

Special Equipment:
Search light, siren, speaker, infrared cameras

The R44 is made by the Robinson Helicopter Company, based in California. The firm was founded in 1973 and now makes more than three hundred helicopters each year.

SUPER HUEY HELICOPTER

The Super Huey helicopter was first used by the U.S. Army. In the 1970s, fire departments in the United States began buying these helicopters and changing them so they could be used to control raging forest fires.

Did You Know?

Huey helicopters were originally called HU-1 Iroquois. This name led to the nickname Huey.

The Super Huey is very large. It has room on board for a nine-person fire crew and all their fire-fighting equipment.

FACTS AND STATS

First Model Year: 1989

Origin: United States

Size of Crew: 9 people

Length:
57 feet (17.4 m)

Height:
13 feet (4.1 m)

Weight:
2 tons (2.5 m tons)

Maximum Load:
2.5 tons (2.3 m tons)

Fuel Capacity:
242 gallons (916 l)

Maximum Power: 1,100 hp

Maximum Speed:
138 miles (222 km) per hour

Range:
402 miles (647 km)

When the helicopter has used up its water supply, the pilot finds a water source, such as a river or lake, to refill the tank. The water is sucked up into the tank through a hose.

The Super Huey can hold a lot of fuel, and it can also carry a large amount of water or foam.

P-3 ORION AIR TANKER

P-3 Orion air tankers are old military aircraft that have been adapted to carry huge tanks of **fire retardant**. These planes are used to help control forest fires. They fill up at airbases and head for the scene of a fire to drop thousands of gallons of retardant on the blaze.

The pilot tries to drop the fire retardant in a line. This line acts as a barrier to stop the fire from spreading.

The tank that holds the fire retardant is located beneath the plane's body. Computer-controlled doors open to drop the retardant.

Did You Know?

The P-3 Orion is named after a group of stars called Orion, the Great Hunter.

FACTS AND STATS

First Model Year: 1990

Origin: United States

Size of Crew: 15 people

Length: 117 feet (35.6 m)

Wingspan: 100 feet (30.5 m)

Height: 38 feet (11.8 m)

Weight:
48 tons (43.4 m tons)

Maximum Load:
22 tons (20 m tons)

Maximum Takeoff Weight:
105,520 pounds (47,855 kg)

Retardant Tank Capacity:
3,000 gallons (11,356 l)

Maximum Power: 2,500 hp

Maximum Speed:
411 miles (661 km) per hour

Takeoff Distance Required:
4,265 feet (1,300 m)

The P-3 was originally designed as a spy plane. The fire-fighting version has wings low on the body and four **turbine** engines with four-blade propellers.

FIRE DART FIREBOAT

Fireboats are powerful fire-fighting machines that patrol large harbors and rivers. The Fire Dart is located on the Thames River in London, England. It is one of the lightest and quickest fireboats ever built.

A **deck monitor** is used to shoot water in a high stream onto a fire. Fire Dart can throw an amazing 475 gallons (1,800 l) of water into the air every minute.

FIRE &

Teams of fireboats and fire-fighting **tugboats** often work together to put out ship fires. The boats never have a shortage of water, because they take water from the sea.

FACTS AND STATS

First Model Year: 1999

Origin: Britain

Size of Crew: 9 people

Length:
46 feet (14 m)

Width:
14 feet (4.3 m)

Height:
9 feet (3 m)

Weight:
13,230 pounds (6,000 kg)

Maximum Load:
24,255 pounds (11,000 kg)

Fuel Capacity:
1,057 gallons (4,000 l)

Maximum Power: 730 hp

Maximum Speed: 30 knots

Two massive engines power the boat through the water. Together, they provide more than 700 horsepower!

ATLANTIC 75 LIFEBOAT

The Atlantic 75 is used to rescue people as far as 50 miles (80 km) out to sea. This lifeboat has a glass-reinforced plastic **hull** topped by an inflatable tube called a **sponson**. It is called a rigid-hull **inflatable** boat.

The hull and sponson are divided into compartments, so the boat will not sink if one section is pierced.

The first rigid-hull inflatable lifeboat was designed by Britain's Royal National Lifeboat Institution in the early 1960s. This kind of boat is now used all over the world to rescue people.

The outboard motors are **immersion-proof.** If the lifeboat capsizes, the motors begin working again as soon as it has flipped back over the right way.

HH-60J JAYHAWK

Air-sea rescue helicopters are used to rescue people at sea. The pilot holds the helicopter in position while a rescue worker is lowered, by a winch, 66 to 98 feet (20 to 30 m). After rescue, the victim can be rushed to the nearest hospital. The HH-60J Jayhawk is used by the U.S. Coast Guard.

Did You Know?

The Jayhawk's design is based on an old helicopter called the VS-300. Built by Russian-born American engineer Igor Sikorsky, the VS-300 first flew in 1939.

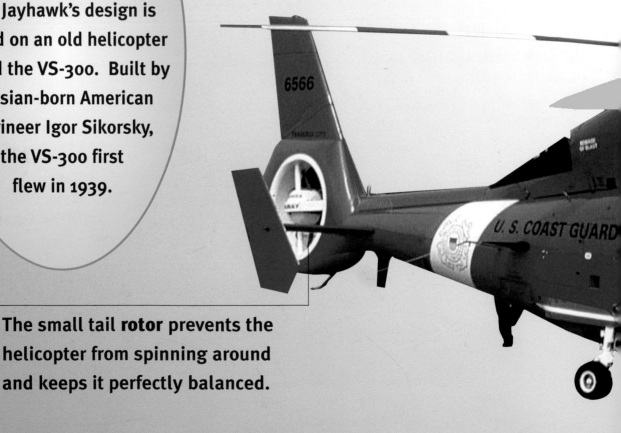

The small tail **rotor** prevents the helicopter from spinning around and keeps it perfectly balanced.

The Jayhawk has a **satellite navigation** system. It tells the pilot the exact location of the helicopter, as well as where the people in need of help are located.

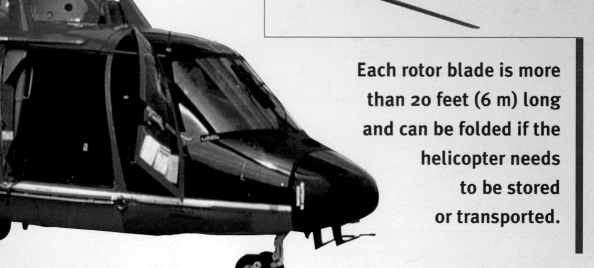

Each rotor blade is more than 20 feet (6 m) long and can be folded if the helicopter needs to be stored or transported.

LR7 RESCUE SUBMERSIBLE

Perry Slingsby Systems is one of the world's leading makers of rescue **submersibles**. These machines are used to rescue people in disabled submarines. The LR7 is the company's new submersible and will replace the LR5.

The LR7 rescue submersible's rear rescue chamber can hold up to twenty-one people.

Did You Know?

The LR7 is fitted with **sonar**. Sonar uses sound waves to tell the crew where to go in the deep, dark ocean.

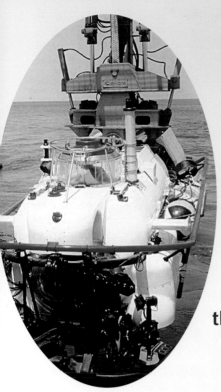

In 2001, the LR5 was used in an attempt to free the crew of a Russian submarine called the *Kursk*. Unfortunately, the LR5 arrived too late to help the Russian sailors.

When the LR7 reaches a submarine, it attaches a special piece called a transfer skirt onto the escape hatch. Once the transfer skirt is attached, the trapped sailors can move safely to the LR7.

HAGGLUNDS BV206

The Hagglunds BV206 is an all-terrain vehicle built in Sweden. This machine is used for many kinds of jobs, including arctic rescue, fire fighting, and disaster relief. The BV206 even floats, so it can travel in water.

Did You Know?

The BV206 is also used for desert exploration, jungle exploration, and even as a snow taxi for tourists.

Hagglunds BV206s are extremely adaptable vehicles. They can operate in snow, ice, mud, water, grass, and sand.

This vehicle is made by the German firm Kassbohrer. It can rescue people trapped in snowdrifts by using its plow attachment to move snow out of the way.

FACTS AND STATS

First Model Year: 1994

Origin: Sweden

Size of Crew: 2 people

Rescue Capacity: 10 people

Length: 23 feet (7 m)

Width: 6.5 feet (2 m)

Height: 8 feet (2.4 m)

Weight: 5 tons (4.5 m tons)

Maximum Load:
2.8 tons (2.5 m tons)

Fuel Capacity:
24 gallons (91 l)

Maximum Power: 136 hp

Maximum Speed:
32 miles (51 km) per hour on land and 1.9 miles (3 km) per hour in water

The vehicle's rear car can be converted into an ambulance unit or a troop carrier in just a few minutes.

MARINE PROTECTOR

The Marine Protector Class coastal patrol boat is a fast, powerful boat that can operate in rough seas. The U.S. Coast Guard uses this patrol boat for catching drug smugglers and other criminals, and it also uses the boat for search and rescue missions.

The **pilot house** has special equipment to help crew members do their jobs. This equipment includes satellite navigation and an **autopilot**. The pilot house also has plenty of windows to allow the crew to see in all directions.

U.S. COAST GUARD

A small, diesel-powered boat is kept at the back of the patrol boat. It is launched and recovered on a specially designed ramp. Only one person is required on deck for launch and recovery.

87325

This boat is known as a cutter. A cutter is a type of U.S. Coast Guard boat that is at least 65 feet (20 m) in length.

GLOSSARY

aerial: relating to something above ground.

autopilot: an operational system that steers a vehicle without a pilot or driver.

battery pack: a portable unit that provides the means for producing electrical power.

body: the main part of a vehicle, where the driver and passengers sit.

boom: a long, extending arm.

cabin: a room in a ship used as living quarters; the part of a plane that houses the pilot, passengers, and cargo.

capsizes: flips over in the water.

crane: a machine used for lifting, using cables attached to a boom.

deck monitor: a water cannon attached to the deck, or top platform, of a fireboat, and which is used to throw a powerful jet of water at a fire.

engine: the part of a vehicle where fuel is burned to create energy.

fire retardant: special chemicals dropped onto a fire to stop the fire from spreading.

foam: frothy chemical substances used for a specific purpose, such as extinguishing a fire.

horsepower: a unit of measurement for an engine's power that was originally based on the pulling strength of a horse.

hull: the main body of a boat or ship, consisting of the bottom and the sides below the deck.

immersion-proof: protected from water damage, even when completely submerged in the water.

inflatable: can be filled with air.

infrared camera: a camera that can record images at night.

knots: units of measurement for the speed of a boat or ship. One knot is equal to 1.15 miles (1.85 km) per hour.

outriggers: long metal bars sticking out from the sides of a vehicle, with feet that rest on the ground to keep the vehicle from tipping over.

pilot house: the part of a ship where the controls are located and where the ship is steered and navigated.

remote control: a device used to operate a machine from a distance.

rotor: a set of spinning blades that lifts a helicopter into the air or controls it during flight.

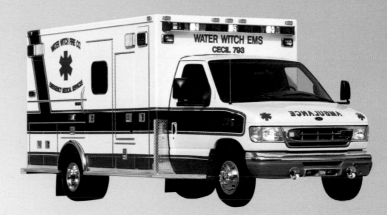

satellite navigation: a system for pinpointing an exact location using information from satellites.

sonar: a system for detecting the location of underwater objects by bouncing sound waves off of them.

sponson: an air-filled tube that helps to stabilize a boat on the water.

submersibles: small underwater vehicles often used for research or rescue.

tugboats: water vehicles used to pull or push ships.

turbine: a machine with a wheel or rotor driven by water, steam, or gases.

winch: a machine that lifts or pulls something by means of a line or cable winding around a reel.

INDEX